HALTED BY THE HOLOCAUST

Alison Spriggs

ISBN: 978-1-910205-59-4

Copyright 2015
Alison Spriggs

First Edition

Printed by
FOR THE RIGHT REASONS CHARITY
60 Grant Street, Inverness, IV3 8BS
Tel: 01463 718844 or 07717457247
Email: fortherightreasons@rocketmail.com
www.fortherightreasons.net

HALTED BY THE HOLOCAUST

Alison Spriggs

Personal accounts, reflections and poetry, challenging
you to stop and think

"To be a voice for those who couldn't speak out, yet their blood cries out, like the blood of Abel."

Alison Spriggs

Acknowledgments

I am gratefully indcbtcd to so many people, who helped me make this book possible.

Thank you to my husband, Stephen and daughter Rachel, for all their patience and encouragement.

Thank you to Galya for all your helpful advice, your honesty, your friendship and for writing the foreword.

Thank you to my faithful proof readers for all your hard work, especially my Dad.

Thank you to all those at For the Right Reasons, especially, Richard, Kevin and Stewart for putting this book together.

Thank you to Helina Birenbaum for her inspiration and courage to share her story, which I would wholeheartedly recommend you read, "Hope is the last to die."

Special thanks to Miriam and to Stefaina, who have shared their personal experiences, I feel exceptionally privileged that you have allowed them to be included in this book.

Finally, thank you to you, the reader for doing me the honour of reading this book.

Alison Spriggs

PREFACE

2015 marks the 70th anniversary of the liberation of Auschwitz. The harrowing evils of the Holocaust must never be forgotten. The Nazi onslaught against the Jews was nothing short of attempted ethnocide and it is imperative that we never, ever forget. This book, therefore, is a timely reflection that serves to commemorate and honour the memory of the millions of Jews who were annihilated during the Second World War.

I have read countless books about the Holocaust and find Alison Spriggs' 'Halted by the Holocaust' to be unique. It provides an historical overview as well as testimonies from those who witnessed and survived the atrocities. Further, this book is also framed by the personal journey of the author which is reflected through her poignant insights and poems that are the fruit of her deep understanding and empathy. The multi-faceted nature of this book makes it accessible to a variety of readers and serves to establish it as a necessary and significant resource for those wishing to learn more about the Holocaust.

The poetry included in 'Halted by the Holocaust' is raw and emotive. The poems transport us to those infamous gates of Auschwitz and seat us alongside the Jewish families within the trains headed to the concentration camps. We can almost hear the cries of horror and smell the stench of death. Simultaneously the author is able to sensitively weave in a sense of hope by drawing the reader to look ahead and, at times, to look above. Alison Spriggs takes us on a journey through her poetry and we come out on the other side more aware, deeply affected and determined to never forget.

This book not only remembers the millions of Jews who perished at the hands of the Nazis but also allows the reader to glimpse miraculous tales of survival and escape first-hand. One such account shared in this book for the very first time will lead the reader from the ashes of the graveyard of Europe to a new life and hope in the reborn state of Israel, where she joined other survivors seeking refuge in their ancient ancestral homeland.

We should all be halted by the Holocaust. We should all be made to stop and think. This book provides us with an opportunity to do just that.

Galya Tregenza

South African Zionist Federation Media Team

Introduction

Who am I, even to attempt to broach this subject?

All that I have read, seen on documentaries, at museums, concentration camps and heard from survivors, will never even equate to one second of the reality of the sheer horror, terror and unspeakable cruelty that those victims of the Holocaust were forced to endure and are still suffering the effects today.

I will never forget those who faced their deaths with such dignity and will respectfully remember those who lost their lives and those who survived the evil brutality of the Holocaust.

What would they say to this generation if they could speak to us today?

What lessons can we learn and what can we do to ensure this does not happen again?

I am endeavouring to share my own personal thoughts and poems in the hope that you too will as I did, stop, and think, reflect, question and pursue a quest for the truth.

Alison Spriggs September 2015

CONTENTS

CHAPTER ONE

I'm sure I would have been taught about the Holocaust at school, but I guess I was so self absorbed in my own problems and was sinking academically that I seemed to have retained very little in my 11 years of education.

I remember having an awareness about it, which was heightened when a very dear friend of mine who was working for a charity in Israel, set up a project, working with Holocaust survivors.

She was a highly intelligent girl, who could have been pursuing a high flying career, but instead chose to volunteer and serve those displaced people who had lost everything and everyone, just because they were Jewish by birth.

Being someone who is passionate about justice, I had great admiration for my friend and was very moved by the experiences she shared when she visited me.

At the time I was working with young people who were disengaged from school and one such pupil's life was completely transformed by a trip to see Auschwitz concentration camp.

The change in her was so astounding to me, that I

vowed that one day I would visit Auschwitz for myself, to try in some way to capture what it was that brought about this miracle.

Angel From The Ashes

A genocide that happened
It seemed so long ago
Is taught to younger pupils
In order that they know
One's suffering behind closed doors
Explodes, can't take it anymore!
Her behaviour is not accepted
Once again she is rejected!
Her wounds of sorrow they did gape
Still on her visit to escape
At Auschwitz camp, went through its gates
To mass suffering, it penetrates
Feeling overwhelmed, intense
breaks the walls of her defence!
Determination fills her mind
To fight for justice and be kind!
Embracing her new identity
She ministers to humanity!

Months later I began to write poetry and wrote a couple of books in aid of Diabetes UK.

Having got my creative appetite whetted, I got involved with the Polish/UK creative writing group. Here, as a group, we published two books that were inspired by Polish literature. This caused me to delve into Polish history, in order to do some research to inspire my contributions.

Julian Tuwim was the first writer I studied and he was born into a Jewish family, involved in the theatre and in arts and is perhaps one of the best well known Polish poets.

Somehow he managed to escape the war and attack on the Jews by emigrating to the United States till 1949. In his writings it was evident that there was a deterioration in his mental health as many of his family perished at the hands of the Nazis.

Julian Tuwim

Changed By Circumstance

War twists what is wrong to make it right
Fellow man I'm forced to fight
Anti Semitic songs in my ears are ringing
Twisting the roots of my upbringing
I'm forced to deny my Jewish line
So a piled body wouldn't be mine
The mask of a new identity's worn
My faith and morals now are torn
Not by circumstance or choice are led
For fear of being numbered with the dead
My expressions of evil, lust and dark
This war for me has left its mark!
So bless these people to let God know
It's in His hands, I must let go.

Now 2015 hails the 70th anniversary of the Holocaust. The term, 'Holocaust' didn't actually come into being until the 1970s, as over time more and more of the immensity of the mass horror unfolded.

Several documentaries were shown; various survivors were interviewed, everyone moving me to tears.

Nothing however prepared me for the documentary about the Liberation of Bergen Belsen, which I will go into further details about later.

It was in attempting to deal with the horrific images that haunted my mind from this documentary, that I began to pour it all out on paper, which in essence laid the foundation for this book.

CHAPTER TWO

There have been various incidents throughout history of wars and genocide, none on quite the scale of the Holocaust, which was described by Winston Churchill as, "The worst worldwide massacre in our history."

The Nazi – Holocaust was birthed from Anti-Semitism, the hatred of Communism and democracy.

The Nazis, under their founder and leader, Adolf Hitler, were growing at a tremendous rate and had two million members by 1933.

The Germans, fell under the spell of this evil dictator, believing his ideology, that they were a superior race, and in an attempt to create what he deemed to be a perfect society, the quest was on to eradicate those deemed impure, the Jews, Slavs, Gypsies, homosexuals and others.

Hitler was born in Linz in Austria from an affair his father had with his niece. His grandfather's name was blank on his father's birth certificate and this alone would have failed to meet with his own ideals!

He went to great efforts to conceal his past, as in those days even having a child out of wedlock was considered a very shameful thing.

Like his father, Hitler himself had relations with his niece and at the same time he got involved with Eva Brown. His heartbroken niece committed suicide when she found out!

Hitler engineered 20th century paganism, with his words; "Neither Catholic nor Protestant has any future left, at least not for the Germans. Nothing will stop me stamping out Christianity in Germany, root and branch. One is either a Christian or a German, you cannot be both.....The clergy will be made to dig their own graves. They will betray their God to us!"

The Germans began building the first concentration camps in Germany in 1933, Dachau being the first of many camps.

Dachau was the training ground for the SS, whose motto was, "We carry the death's head on our cap as a warning to our enemies and an indication to our Fuhrer that we will sacrifice our lives for his idea!"

Floggings were given on a regular basis to prisoners for the most trivial things, like failing to salute properly, when almost collapsing with hunger and exhaustion!

The victims would be flogged for a period, and then left in a cell with a knife and a noose to encourage them to commit suicide. If they failed to do so, the floggings went on and the process was repeated until the victim either died or killed themselves.

Another extreme form of torture used was pawl hanging, which involved stripping the victims and tying their hands behind their backs and their feet together and hanging them for an hour by their hands. This was excruciatingly painful and when they were taken down they were made to salute which they couldn't do, so they were then flogged.

Germany invaded Poland on the 1st September 1939. The occupation of Poland was followed by aggression against other countries, which led to the majority of Europe being occupied by Germany.

In April 1940 the German army attacked and occupied Denmark and Norway.

In May 1940, they attacked Belgium, Holland and Luxembourg and then started occupying France.

A Christian, Dutch watch maker and his family, by the name of "Ten-Boom" hid Jewish people in their homes, as they could not ignore what was going on and do nothing, believing in the words from scripture:

"Rescue those being led away to death; hold back those

staggering towards slaughter. If you say but we knew nothing about this, does not He who weighs the heart perceive it? Does not He who guards your life know it? Will He not repay each person, according to what he has done?"(Proverbs 24v11)

He and all his family were either killed or lost their lives in concentration camps, when their actions were discovered, except the watchmaker's daughter Corrie (see picture.) She, instead of choosing to be bitter, chose to be better and went on to share an inspiring message of her faith, hope, love and forgiveness in various countries. Her story has been made into both a book and a film, called "The Hiding Place."

In April 1941, the Germans turned on Yugoslavia and Greece and in June 1941, they struck their allies, the Soviet Union.

Following the outbreak of World War 2, the Germans began building various concentration camps in the countries they now occupied.

The camps were run directly by the SS, under the command of Heinrich Himmler, who referred to the Jews as, "Sub humans, emotionally and spiritually inferior to animals!"

On watching a documentary about him recently, he described the Jews as a people who had become "International with their businesses therefore had to be stopped!"

In this day and age, businesses are aspiring to be international and their enterprising skills would be encouraged. They would be esteemed and considered highly successful! What a generation of skilled and talented people the world has missed out on!

Following the invasion of Poland, life became increasingly difficult for Polish Jews and subsequently for all Jews in the remaining parts of Europe that the Germans were occupying.

There were signs outside shops, cafes, cinemas and theatres saying, "NO JEWS ALLOWED!" Jewish businesses were boycotted and vandalised, they were in fear of going out as they risked being beaten or even shot!

Nobody could leave the country without paying the "Reichsfluchtsteuer," which was a hefty tax imposed on the Jews, rather like what the IS are doing to Christians in the Middle East today.

If they could afford this tax, they were unable to access any money, as Jewish real estate had been confiscated and Jewish bank accounts could no longer be accessed by their owners, leaving them in an impossible situation.

This was followed by a notice for all Jews to be evicted from their homes, with just seven hours' notice, with a limit on the belongings they could take. Failure to comply carried the threat of serious consequences!

Jews were then marched or transported to the nearest ghetto, a sectioned off part of the poorest area of the city. Its inhabitants were forced out of their homes, to make way for the ghetto, which incited further hatred towards the Jews.

One eye witness account remembers a Jewish man of about sixty, in a postman's uniform, stumbling and a youth of about eighteen trying to help him up. The S.S coldly shot him, the dying man's eyes were fixed on the youth who had tried to save him, the despair in the youth's eyes as he cried, "Oh father!"

The S.S assassin calmly took out a cigarette and because of the wind, took several attempts to light it. It seemed much easier for him to destroy a human life than to light a cigarette!

On our recent visit to Poland in April 2015, we stayed in Kazimierz, the Jewish quarter of Krakow and visited the old ghetto.

The walls of the ghetto were built to replicate Jewish tombstones to give the impression that they were surrounded by death and part of the wall still remains today.

Inside the ghetto, up to eight families would have to occupy one room, with no privacy. Cramped in poor conditions, disease quickly broke out and if it hadn't been for Tadeusz Pankiewicz the pharmacist, who risked his life by smuggling much needed medications into this particular ghetto, many more lives would have been lost. This is a eye witness account from a Polish lady, Stefania Napiorkowska, who has very kindly allowed

me to share her story: "I was born and raised in Lodz
and I still live there today. Before the Second World War
my family, my parents, my younger sister Regina and I
lived at 74 Lagiewnicka Street.

In 1940, the Germans started to create a Jewish ghetto,
from Polnocna Street to Stefana Street and further to
Doly. The area was closed but you could buy a ticket for
five pfennigs in the ticket machine at Nowomiejska
Street, just beside the ghetto and get a tram to go
through it, to Julianow.

We had to move out from our flat at Lagiewnicka Street
as it became a part of the ghetto. We moved into our
cousin's flat, at Okopowa Street. Dad said that the war
will be over soon and we would come back to our flat,
but it lasted six long years and we never returned there.
Along the centre line of the Okopowa Street there was a
barbed-wired fence, the Poles lived on one side and the
Jews on the other.

I have a lot of memories connected to the Second World
War, but some of them are most vivid and most
terrifying. I remember like it was yesterday, it was a
beautiful warm day and I saw a couple of young Jews,
walking alongside the ghetto fence. A German gendarme
called to them: "Komm hier, komm hier!" Then he hit
the girl in her chest with his machine gun, and then he
hit the boy. They both fell down. The German then told

them to get up and stand by the fence. Then he shot them. I saw it through the window, hiding behind a curtain so the gendarme could not see me because he could shoot me – that was life during the war."

One of the most famous heroes for a fortunate few of the occupants of the ghetto was Oscar Schindler, his story made famous by Stephen Spielberg's film, "Schindler's List."

Being a respected associate of Himmler, Schindler's factory became an approved workplace for the Jews. Unlike any other of the work places, that enforced hard slave labour, Schindler treated his work force with respect and he provided for their basic needs. When he heard about the death camps he devised a plan to save his work force and those of their families that he could, saving a thousand Jews from the gas chambers.

Oscar Schindler

Oscar Schindler, a man of conscience
 Rare to find in men of his day
He had core values
Sadly shared by few
He respected the effort
And loyalty of the Jew
He couldn't turn a blind eye

Follow the rules
Condemn them to die
At his factory fear was left at the door
The hungry were fed
With some left to store
Fathering them like Abraham
Investing his all
To outwit the enemy,
He made up a list
Of all names known
Of those condemned to die
Now granted salvation
What a joy to be on that list
Like being on Heaven's list
Where you wouldn't perish
But have everlasting life!

Oscar Schindler's desk

A famous heroine of the ghetto was Irena Sendler, who was a Polish social worker, who smuggled babies out of the ghetto and found foster homes for them, even managing to reunite the few remaining parents who survived with their children at the end of the war in 1945.

A Tribute to Irena Sendler

Irena Sendler, a Polish girl so very brave
Two thousand, five hundred children did save
A social worker, you took a stand
And entered the ghetto to give a hand

You made a difference, did what you could
And amongst all this evil, you did good
When you knew they were all to die
You risked your life and questioned, "Why?"

Smuggled babies out in boxes topped with bricks
You thought of various plans and tricks!
You found new parents for each kid
And kept their details in a jar with a lid

Hoping if an end came to their plight
Back with their parents, you'd reunite
Though you are caught, and tortured so bad
You wouldn't give away the details you had

The Gestapo took you off to be shot
You were rescued from that terrible plot
Each child you did protect and defend
Until the war finally came to an end

The ones that returned were very few
An eternal ache in the heart of each Jew
Minds with shocking memories piled
But thanks to Irena they got their child!

You courageously saved a new generation
A remnant of God's own chosen nation

CHAPTER THREE

Due to the cramped, disease-ridden conditions in the ghettos, the Jews were becoming increasingly desperate. Seizing an opportunity to exploit their situation even further, the Gestapo fabricated a cruel deception.

For those who could afford it they would move them on to far more superior accommodation. With a false sense of hope in their hearts many Jews willingly handed over all their money and jewellery, and then gathered together their few remaining belongings with the promise of a new start.

When the cattle trains arrived for them, they were instructed to leave their belongings behind and they would be sent on later, but weren't. The Gestapo looted what remained and what nobody wanted was left strewn on the square of the ghetto!

Today a poignant memorial is in the square of empty chairs standing alone depicting how they must have felt, empty and out of place!

Musical Chairs

Life is like a game of musical chairs,
You that focused on your own success
You fail to notice
That one by one, everyone is disappearing
One day there will no longer be
A vacant seat for you in this world
And you too will be taken

Time to take notice
Before you meet the One
Who sits on the great chair above
Controlling the music

When the cattle trains arrived, people were herded on, and when there was no room for more, the Gestapo fired shots at the entrance, causing them to jump back which made room for some more!

People had to travel various distances, the average journey lasting the day and the night. The longest journey was for those who came from Greece. Their journey took two weeks and a large number of them died before reaching their destination.

There was a lack of air, no sanitation facilities, little or no water and occasionally a stale piece of bread, if you were fortunate!

On the occasion when water or bread was offered, it was given in exchange for a demanded amount of jewellery, watches or any few items of value they had left in their possession. The Gestapo were not concerned for individuals and when people tried to alert them to a death on the train, they were often met with a stern reply of, "Keep your corpse, you will soon have many more!"

The carriages became like large mobile coffins and the S.S became heirs of their riches!

These trains were between thirty to fifty carriages long, each carriage was designed to fit a maximum of up to eight horses.

The following account is a description of a journey on one of these cattle trains by a survivor:

"The normal load for trains was sixty to ninety people; there were one hundred and twenty on the train I was on. We had two buckets for our human needs, we had to overcome our inhibitions to use them – men, women, strangers, and children – but we used them and they weren't sufficient for one hundred and twenty!

Anyway, with every jolt of the train, the muck ran out, so we were sitting in it and we couldn't do a thing about it! This was in June, a very hot summer and there was very little air in the train. The two only openings had barbed wire over them and the air became really unbearable! We were so thirsty, we had a bottle of water to drink, we had drunk that on the first day, thinking we would get a refill but this never happened and we were getting more and more thirsty! In our normal life we talk about being thirsty, but thirsty there meant one's lips were parched, broken and hurting! You had a stale piece of bread in your hand, but couldn't eat it because you couldn't swallow any more.
It meant people went into hysterics, people went mad, people had heart attacks and people died. We had the

dead, the mad, the hysterical and constant screaming among us and we couldn't do a thing about it!"

Cattle Trains

Cattle trains, hot and crammed with mankind
Homes, belongings and friends left behind
Knowing not their horrid destination

When they climbed aboard at the railway station
They were crushed, jammed in tight
Standing travelling day and night
All are hungry and children cry
With no water, mouths are dry
People sick with the urine smell
When will this end, this journey to hell?
Stiff and sore and some have cramp
As the train rolls into a prison camp
A people that clung to a future hope,
That all went up in Auschwitz smoke

"The train moved off amidst incessant shrieks, cries and rifle shots, our infernal ride to the death camp had started. Panicked people were fighting for every inch of space. The strongest and tallest blocked access to the small window. We had no light or air. The heat and stuffiness intensified our thirst. People collapsed and were trampled on and crushed to death, people raged and people prayed!

Some courageous Poles we passed, hastily drew water from a stream and ran and got a bottle of water into an outstretched hand. Those who were nearest the window got some. It was muddy, smelly and dirty but priceless!"
(Helina Birenbaum – Hope is the last to die)

The Cost Of Mercy

Herded into cattle trains
With whips and guns
Like frightened animals
Squashed but standing together
Shots fired at the door
To make you jump back
And create space for more
Jammed together
Travelled day and night
Suffocating, fighting for air
The awful stench from sweat

And lack of sanitation
The intense dryness and thirst
Every last bit of moisture
Had been sucked out
Would we survive to see our destination?
Many didn't
Hope came in an act of mercy
As Poles, realising our plight
Risked their own lives
To fill containers of water
From the river
And deliver them
To the outstretched grateful hands
Extended from the cattle train
God bless them!

"If anyone gives you even a cup of water because you
belong to the Messiah, I assure you, that person will
be rewarded."
Mark 9v41

The Jews are very passionate about the observation of their feasts and festivals and one such festival is, "Simhath Torah." This is celebrated on the last day of Sukoth, the festival of booths. This is when the yearly cycle of reading the Torah is completed and the next cycle begins.

It is a time of great rejoicing and celebrating, where the sacred Torah scrolls are removed and carried through the synagogue seven times in a joyful procession, with children flying flags, there is singing and dancing and sweets for the children.
It is when the Jews really express their true joy in having the Torah and the delight and privilege they feel at observing the sacred words it contains.

I heard one account of where, on board one of these death trains, a rabbi announced that it was now Simhath Torah. Although they did not have the scrolls, it was discovered that one of the passengers had managed to save a small fragment of the Torah that had been destroyed.

Although they were all cramped, in inhuman conditions and could hardly breath, they danced with the sway of the train, celebrating life, knowing that every motion of the train was taking them closer to their death.

CHAPTER FOUR

When people arrived off the train they were so relieved that their nightmare journey was over but were unaware of the fact that this was just the beginning of their suffering.

Though they did see the emaciated prisoners, a shocking sight, people wrongly understood they must be dangerous prisoners.

The facade was kept up to maintain a level of order, Music would be playing on arrival and ambulances were lined up to meet them, which gave a false sense of reassurance.

When the selection process took place, the aged, the sick and the children were put to the left and males and females were separated.

The cover up being, that the sick were to be taken away to be treated and the physically fit were needed to help with essential work.

Tragically it was at this point that many women lied about elder children's ages, thinking to spare them of work, not realising they were sending them straight to their death and those few who survived carried the guilt of this for the rest of their lives!

Pregnant Jewish women who arrived, went straight to the gas chambers. In order to discover those in early stages of pregnancy, special privileges were promised to those carrying a child, a further evil deception!

There were many concentration camps or, "Arbeitslager," Hitler's occupied Europe was dotted with them.

A very evil man
Hatched a very evil plan
To annihilate the Jews
Fellow man he did confuse
Fueled them up with hate
And they took the bait
Like pawns they played his game
Operating without shame
Uprooted, frightened, starved
Diseased, persecuted and scarred
Caged in conditions not humane
Then piled onto a cattle train
Inhaling the choking fumes of gasses
They met the Messiah in their masses

In Auschwitz alone, there were the 3 large camps, Auschwitz 1, Auschwitz 11-Birkenau and Auschwitz 111-Monowitz, as well as dozens of other smaller sub – camps.

It was not to the promised, more superior accommodation that each train's occupants arrived but one of these hard labour or death camps was their true destination, where the weakest and disadvantaged were the most exposed.

This is the account of a survivor's arrival at Auschwitz:

"The scene around was full of commotion, people were screaming, crying, there were children, there were dogs, there were guards, beating everyone across the head and screaming, "OUT, OUT, OUT!""

When we all jumped out of the train we were put into a long column and told to march forward. It was not a station, no platforms, just these barracks, the barbed wire, nowhere else to go – it really was the end of the line! On the right were these creatures in rags and naked women. I thought: what are they doing here? I will never be like them.

Then I saw some men on the other side in stripped gear. In between all you tried to do was avoid the guards, the sticks and the dogs, so you kept inside the column and marched. You were carried like a flood; it must have been for about a mile. Then three men in uniforms; the uniforms spotless, with boots gleaming like mirrors I'll never forget the impression of the man in the middle, Dr Mengele.

I glanced at him; he was very good looking, not a menacing face at all, although not benevolent. I remember his boots were shiny, he was absolutely immaculate. He had white gloves on, not exactly like a traffic policeman, but a sign of distinction and importance. He lifted his hand as he looked at everybody who went past him and just made a gesture and said, "Right, left, left, left, right, left, left, right....."

This was called the selection process. It happened initially on arrival, where those who looked fit for manual labour were selected and the weak and the ill were taken straight to the gas chambers for the alleged shower, locked in, and gassed to death!
Children were separated from parents, loss, fear and confusion was paramount!"

Questions

Why were we herded like animals
crammed on to a train?
To get to our safe new community houses,
it was insane!
Why paraded so undignified,
naked and bare?
Why some to the left and some to the right?
The ones on the left,
what became of their plight?
Why in the woods
did they build the showers?
Is there a train over there
to these houses of ours?

Longing for a shower
and to get to that station
Unaware,
Heaven was the home
 of their destination
While this was the Hell
 they endured to get there
Those outside the fence,
didn't know? Or didn't care?

CHAPTER FIVE

I'll never forget the day we went to visit Auschwitz – Birkenau in April 2015.

Fortunately we were with an organised tour and on the journey down, we were shown a film of the liberation.

One of the most gruesome parts of the film was where they showed post-mortems being carried out on small children and babies to confirm the cause of death! One boy's corpse was quite black, as he had been poisoned.

There was a tiny baby's corpse, the head almost bigger than its body, the cause of death, severe malnutrition.

The journey was about an hour and a half from Krakow and the camps were located very much in the countryside.

It was strange because suddenly you saw, in this apparently isolated setting, car park, after car park after car park, with hundreds and hundreds of coaches!

There were huge queues at the entrance, but fortunately, being with a pre - arranged tour, we didn't have to queue!

When we got in it was very much like the scene of an airport terminal! There were very strict limits on what you could carry, just one very small handbag, which was searched! You had to remove your jacket, watch, shoes and put them on a tray, which went through the scanner and then you walked through the scanner one at a time, just like at the airport!

My daughter set the beeper off, with the press studs on her sweatshirt, and was subjected to a body search! This whole process was unexpected and gave it quite a military feel! We were introduced to our guide and given headphone sets, so the whole group could hear him.

There were literally hundreds of tour groups of all different nationalities being shown round when we were there! The camps are massive, when you think of the thousands of people who lived there at any one time!

It was snowing, which added to the chilling, bleak atmosphere, as we entered the gates, bearing the words, "ARBEIT MACHT FREI" which means, "Work brings freedom!" Another Nazi deception!

Where was this freedom
These gates spoke of as we entered?
Suitcases, no labels of holiday locations,
Looted by the enemy, stacked up
Destination death camp
The end of their journey!

Piles of shoes
Ones bought for dancing
That never reached the dance floor
The Jewish cobbler ne'er foresaw
All his hard work dumped
On this God forsaken heap!

Hair, once beautiful
Brushed and braided
Now shaved off
Their innocent victims
To make into mattresses!

Spectacles carefully measured
And fitted by the local optician,
Now with no ears left to hang from
And no eyes left to aid!

The teeth of the rich
Removed by force
Not in decay but,
Without anesthetic
Creating excruciating pain
But not as much as in their hearts!

Beyond the gates
Where freshing up meant
To wash yourself with soap
Made from the bones
Of your dead brothers and sisters!

Beneath the ground
Are stories of unsung heroes
Where one day their victory
Will be celebrated
Where they will experience true freedom
Beyond Heaven's gates!

In Auschwitz 1, there was a room piled high with
thousands and thousands of glasses, and a room filled
with all the suitcases, a room piled high full of
people's shoes and perhaps the most disturbing of all
was the room which contained all the human hair
shaved off their innocent victims to make their
bedding!

We went to the area where they did the morning and evening roll call. This is where all prisoners were counted. If any prisoner tried to escape they were shot and twelve other prisoners from their barracks were hanged at roll call as a stark warning to the others!

At times they were issued with postcards they could send to loved ones. They had to state that they were in good health and being well looked after and they were given a false destination that they were to say they were at.

This had a twofold purpose, firstly to give details of the whereabouts of others, especially the Jews, in order that they too could be captured, and secondly to encourage them to come.

When the workers were no longer useful they were dispatched to the gas chambers, as simple and as cold blooded as that!

The sun shines brightly
People respond to its warmth
Discarding their outer garments
Captivated and cheered by its appearance
Behind the high barb wire fence
Working in the blistering unbearable heat
On one side of the fence
Well toned bodies sunbathing, relaxing
On the other side
Tortured, wizened frames are collapsing.

At roll call they were paraded, mainly naked in all weathers in front of the evil Dr Mengele, otherwise known as Dr Death, who was in charge of the selection process. Everyone had to be present at role call, even if they had pneumonia or scarlet fever.

If a person looked fit for hard labour at a glance, they were spared, if not they were sent to their death!

Dr Mengele was also on the lookout for specimens on which to conduct his horrific experiments. He had a particular interest in twins and dwarfs.

Victims were tied to tables and used for experiments to graft bones and muscles, without anaesthetic or antiseptic!

He would test how long it took for death to come when a person was immersed in iced water and also in scalding water of various temperatures, and how long a person would survive just drinking salt water!

His so-called scientific experiments were sadistic torture rather than a medical quest for truth!

Poisons were injected into people to see how they reacted and how long it would take them to die, men were castrated, women sterilised or artificially inseminated, and he even experimented in performing sex change operations, all against the person's wishes and without anaesthetic, generally causing them to die a very painful death.

These experiments were carried out in block 10 and people knew that when you went in there, it generally meant that you wouldn't be coming out!

The twins

I clung to Mum frightened, my twin clung to me
Swamped, but alone in a forsaken Jewish sea
Mother, crying out Papa's name, shouting my brothers
Gone and lost forever, like many others

As twins we were selected for medical experiments
Pumped with pills and pricked with sharp implements
Sick with rashes, our small bodies would swell
A doctor would write notes, but never us tell

Hannah, in the next bed soon became my friend
Till it was all over and in death it did end
I missed my Papa, I wanted him so bad
He always knew how to cheer up the sad

Then I remembered what Papa taught us to say
I shut my eyes tight and began to pray
I knew that my prayer was answered that day
Some good soldiers came and took us away

Back to our mother we were returned
Up from the woods, the chimney it burned
"Don't look dears," Was what Mother said
As we had to go past those naked and dead

CHAPTER SIX

Life in the concentration camps was full of never ending fear, cruelty, starvation and depravity.
On arrival, if they passed the initial selection, they were stripped and made to go through a most undignified examination!

A number was then tattooed on their arm as if to rob them of their identity and reduce them to a mere number.

Those with the lower numbers were socially above those with the higher numbers because they had lived more days in a place where nobody wanted to live and thus had created a privilege!

To add to the humiliation they went through, they had their heads shaved, further depriving them of their basic individuality.

Heads completely shaved
Impossible to notice gender
Till the twice daily ritual of roll call
Where these zombie like figures
Face the ongoing humiliation of
Being paraded naked in all weathers
To be counted yet again
Lest one attempts to escape
Then gets shot and
Twelve others hanged as a warning
They pinch their grey cheeks
In a vain attempt to display some colour
Trying hard to disguise their suffering
And appear healthy
So they may pass the selection test
And be spared to see another day.

Those who did not pass the selection, went straight to
their death and were not registered, hence there were
many more people that did perish than were actually
accounted for!

Auschwitz 11-Birkenau, the second of three parts of
the Auschwitz camp, had more than 90,000 people
crammed into it in 1944 and a total of 200,000 in all
three camps!

A typical day consisted of, roll call, with little or no clothes, to go through the selection process, wondering if today you would remain alive to get through the day, pass the selection process, avoid the bullets the SS fired, often for no reason, tormented by grief for those you had lost and constantly worrying about the fate of loved ones from whom you had become separated.

Hunger was your constant companion, gnawing at you and eating away at you piece by piece, till you were so emaciated your feeble frame could barely carry you.

Some dark brownish hot liquid, it was hard to distinguish if it was tea or coffee, was distributed in the morning and very watery soup for your mid-day meal and a dry crust of black bread in the evening, which irritated gums that were made sensitive due to malnutrition. This was all you had to sustain you and there was little, if any nourishment in that!

The soup was the same, mainly water and turnips and all sorts of uneatable items could be found in it. Hair, dead lice, even the occasional mouse or rat!

Those whose job it was to carry the food were called, "Esskommando."

Bowls to be used for soup were shared and because they were shot if they tried to go to the toilet out with the permitted times of twice daily, many desperate people resorted to using the bowls as chamber pots and the same bowls were then used for soup!

In the women's camps the S.S dosed their food with a chemical to stop their menstruation.

Then you had your twice daily supervised trip to the toilet facilities, It consisted of a long barn like structure, containing a very long bench with two very long rows of holes in it side by side and back to back, where people had to sit right next to each other shoulder to shoulder and back to back.

They had a long trough filled with some dirty, cold water to wash in afterwards, no soap, no towels and no toilet roll!

They had a maximum of 10 minutes for them all to complete this process, till the next lot were marched in!

Horrifically, what was considered to be the most privileged position in this camp and everyone wanted to do it, was cleaning the cesspit after all these thousands of people had eventually used it! The reason being that they had some shelter from the weather and the most important privilege was that they could use the facilities when they required and in a bit more privacy!

Those whose job it was to clean the toilet facilities were referred to as, "Scheisskommando."
Following the toilet ordeal, they were sent to work, doing various types of hard manual labour, for a full eleven hour shift!

Examples of work could be building railways, digging trenches to bury the remains of the deceased, stripping the bodies of those who had been gassed, shaving their hair, gathering their shoes and clothes and sorting them.

The biggest work group then was the, "Sonderkommando," They supervised those condemned to the gas chambers as they undressed, and sent their belongings to another group to be sorted out and disinfected before being sent to Germany. Their main duties were to remove the naked bodies and burn them at the crematorium on SS orders!

Other groups went round and piled the corpses of those who had died previously into heaps. Death was surrounding them, the stench of death and decaying flesh continually filling their nostrils!
Individual acts of revolt always brought mass

reprisals, discouraging others from doing the same.

When the working day was finally over, another roll call was carried out, the dry crust of bread issued, the toilet shift, then bed!

They slept on two or three tiered, wooden slatted bunks, 12ft by 5ft, with as many as six or even eight to a bunk, with no mattress. The only type of bedding, if you were fortunate, was the blanket that was made from recycled human hair!

There could be over 900 people in one wooden unit, which was like a large cattle shed. The wooden slatted roof, wasn't fully waterproof or windproof so the earth floor became a sea of mud! It was absolutely freezing in winter, and sweltering in summer!

Latterly these units housed 1,500 and conditions were so cramped that the top tiers of the bunks would collapse, often crushing to death or bringing severe injury to those below!

Disease, infections and head lice swept throughout the camp and as a result many died on a daily basis. It was common place to wake and find a deceased person lying beside you!

The itch

The terrible itch of the parasites
Gorging themselves on the little blood left
In their starved, emaciated bodies
Provides a distraction
From the immense pangs of hunger.
The worry and despair of the next day
And the fate of loved ones
From whom
You have been forcibly separated

CHAPTER SEVEN

Originally those condemned to death at Birkenau were either shot in the forest of Braezinsky or gassed in the infamous "White House" in the camp and the corpses were incinerated in a "death pit."

By the summer of 1941, the German army was virtually in control of Eastern Europe and the implementation of the "Final Solution" began. Mass shootings of Jews and gassing them in gas vans were the initial means used to terminate them. Ironically, because this was having a negative psychological effect on the German soldiers, entertainment evenings were established to boost their morale and a gas chamber was developed to make it easier for them!

This was initially used by Hitler to rid Germany of what he deemed to be imperfection and the most innocent and vulnerable in society, disabled children, were amongst its first victims! This all stemmed from Hitler's firm belief in Darwin's, "Survival of the fittest" theory!

Sophie Scholl, a young children's nurse from Munich, was so incensed and shocked to discover that these lovely precious children she cared for, and had grown to love, were being singled out and taken on a bus to be gassed!

She said that the children, were so excited to be travelling on a bus, thinking they were going on a trip to somewhere nice. Questioned where they were going, the only thing the staff could think to tell them was that they were going to meet Jesus! The children left happy and were singing songs about Jesus!

Sophie, along with her brother, who was too ill to be called up, tried to write to Heads of States to inform them what was going on and also did a letter drop at Munich University in an attempt to gain support, but instead, was arrested, and tried in court, for defending the innocent. She, along with her brother and her friend, were executed!

In December 1941, "Chelmo," the first death camp was established in Poland. It was followed by, Belzec, Treblinka and Sobibor.   Auschwitz and Majdanek served as both concentration and death camps. It was there that the Nazis used the gas chambers efficiently and relentlessly to address what they saw as, "The Jewish Problem!"
`

The original gas chambers and crematorium in Auschwitz were deemed not to have the capacity to carry this out as quickly as they would have liked, so in February 1943 a new, much larger, crematorium and gas chamber was constructed at Auschwitz 11 – Birkenau.

At first Jews and non Jews were sent to the crematorium. After June 1943 the gas chamber and crematory ovens were reserved for Jews and Gypsies, except by reprisal or by mistake.

At Birkenau there were four crematory ovens. The four ovens were heated by thirty fires. Each oven had one hundred and twenty openings in which three corpses could be placed at a time. That meant they could dispose of 17,280 corpses every 24 hours!

The ovens, with murderous efficiency, functioned both day and night!

On inauguration day, 12,000 Polish Jews were put to death as a minor sacrifice to the Nazi god, "Molech!" This god is mentioned in the bible in Leviticus chapter 18 verse 21; "Do not give any of your children to be sacrificed to Molech, for you must not profane the name of your God, I am the Lord." (NIV)

The name, "Birkenau," means, "Birch Forest," a deceptively charming name for such a chilling place! With a name like that, you would think there would be the sound of birds but that is something that strikes you, there are no birds there. Apparently there used to be, prior to the Holocaust, and, as I have heard from many other friends who have visited other death camps, the same is true – no birds!

Memorial Silence

In the death camps
Creation itself
Is silent
No birds
Are allowed
To sing
The heart heaviness
Of the Creator
Is tangible!

This new gas chamber consisted of three areas, the waiting room, the shower room and the ovens. There was a large chimney in the center, there were nine ovens, and the capacity of each oven was two thousand corpses a day!

Many 'people groups' fell short of the Nazi ideal such as political opponents, gypsies, Jehovah's witnesses and homosexuals. They too were sent to the concentration camps and due to the awful conditions and the barbaric treatment, many of them died. It was only the Jews however that were selected for mass extermination!

Ironically, a Star of David was placed above the entrance to the gas chamber and a sign was painted in Hebrew on a purple curtain covering the entrance to the gas chamber that said, "This is the gateway to God. Righteous men will pass through."

On being selected at Birkenau, the Jews were ordered into the first room and told to undress for a shower. They were even given a towel and piece of soap to make this evil deception more credible!

They were then made to enter a large room, with signs encouraging personal hygiene and fake shower heads. When everyone had entered, the airtight doors were locked. Zyclon B, which was a type of cyanide, a greyish blue powder that evaporated into a gas, was poured into valves in the ceiling. Within minutes they would all die and the doors would be opened by the "Sonderkommando," in gas masks. They would extract any gold teeth and shave off hair from anyone who still had any. Then they would put the bodies into the ovens to be burned and the ashes were then used as a fertilizer for fields and vegetable gardens!

Among the many 438,000 Hungarian Jews murdered in Auschwitz-Birkenau, was a Scots woman who died there, Jane Haining. She was a missionary teacher at a Christian mission school in Hungary, she refused to leave the children in her care to suffer alone and died in Birkenau aged 47.

The Nazis tried to destroy the gas chambers at Birkenau as the camp was about to be liberated and they are in ruins, but the gas chambers and crematorium in Auschwitz 1 remains. When we went into it, although the temperature was cold outside, there was a much greater chill felt inside, even with all the people on the various tours inside at the same time!

Outside the gas chamber

The crematorium ovens

Krakow in 1945, as history said
6 million Jews, tortured and dead
Treblinka, now it's been revealed
Another million Hitler concealed
Trusting Jews, packed on each train
Into camps, never seen again
The promise of hope in these ghettos anew
Was the lie that was told to every Jew
Charcoaled bones, ashes, remain of the lost
Museums, memorials mark the Holocaust
How can we ignore the shame of the past?
For the innocent millions of Jews that were gassed.

CHAPTER EIGHT

The word, "Hope" in Hebrew is, "Tikvah," Ha Tikva
(The Hope) is also the name of a Zionist song, which
many of those condemned to death sung on route to
the gas chambers. This song is now Israel's national
anthem.

Ha Tikva

As long as deep in the heart,
The soul of a Jew yearns,
And forward to the East
To Zion, an eye looks
Our hope will not be lost,
The hope of two thousand years,
To be a free nation in our land,
The land of Zion and Jerusalem

(Adapted from a poem by Naphtali Herz)

Even in those appalling conditions and although
everyone was starving to death, so many of the Jews
held fast to their faith and were determined to uphold
their traditions of fasting on Yom Kippur

One woman, who was well respected within the camp, was very ill and as many gathered round her, she told everyone, "Do not be sorry for me, I am going to be with My Lord. We must say goodbye to each other, let's pray."

Silently many other women gathered round her, Protestants, Catholics, Jews, Gentiles and Atheists, all praying together, when the S.S came to take her away!

One night on Simhath Torah, in one of the death camps, a number of Jews gathered together to celebrate Simhath Torah but, just as had happened earlier on the train, they had no sacred scrolls for their procession. The Rabbi went and spoke to a young boy and asked him what he remembered from what he had learned? He remembered Shima Yisrael and much more.

The Rabbi lifted him up and began dancing with him, as though he were the precious Torah and they all joined in! They sang and danced and wept, and, once again, the Simhath Torah was celebrated with vigour and determination!

Rising from the Ashes

We will not be defeated
We will not be destroyed
Determined like an athlete
Competing for a prize

Through betrayal and adversity
Disease, despair and pain
We're rising from the ashes
To live our life again

When this world is silent
Deaf and blinded without sight
We have to bc determined
To carry on the fight

A remnant of Abraham's descent
Fueled by resilience and hope
March from decaying death camps
Our memories up in smoke

This remnant liberated
Although that's very true
Freedom does not seem to last
If you are born a Jew

No home now to return to
They are bombed or occupied
No welcome from the family
Along with friends they've died

Wandering this world like nomads
In our homeless plight
Even in our land of origin
For peace we have to fight

When the final trumpet blows
And Messiah comes again
In the New Jerusalem
Forever peace will reign

When visiting Auschwitz, I purchased a book called,
"Hope is the last to die," By Helina Birenbaum.
Miraculously, Helina, was the only person that I ever
heard of, who actually survived the gas chambers.

This is her account:

"In the middle of the night, the SS noisily threw open the hut door, arousing us with their shouts and beatings. They began herding us out, making sure no one hid or escaped. A fearful confusion ensued. Sleepy and frightened to death, we crowded to the door, pushing and trampling on one another in the darkness and panic. The Storm Troopers ran around like mad dogs. They made us form fours, lit electric lamps, swore and counted us. They were taking us to the crematorium! The terrible news fell on us like a thunderbolt and spread like lightning through the ranks.

My heart beat rapidly. I could not believe it. Once again, as months earlier, on the Warsaw Umschlag, when the Nazis set up a machine-gun in front of us, I could not believe death was possible and I did not yield to the general despair.

The SS gave an order and we moved off in the direction of the crematorium, some women were weeping, others were tearing their hair, praying or bidding farewell to their mothers or sisters. They herded us into a hut, the interior of which resembled a bath-house. Despite the darkness, we observed stacks of empty gas containers on the ground in front of the hut. There was a strange sweetish odor in the air. There was no doubt now that they were taking us to execution. The women went out of their minds, they groaned, wailed and had convulsions.

They herded us into this bath-house and barred the door behind us. Now we had to carry out the order given previously, to undress and hang our clothes up on hooks on the walls. Obediently we undressed in silence. We knew there was no way out. We hung our clothes up, and then sat down on benches along the walls, waiting in extreme agitation. When and how would death come?

Time passed. Hour followed hour. But nothing happened and no one came. It was silent both inside and outside the bath-house. Perhaps they had forgotten us? A faint hope slowly began emerging. Towards morning, they came back, and after the nightmare of waiting for death in the gas chamber, we went outside. They counted us again (as though anyone could have escaped from that locked building!), and took us back to the men's camp, to the same hut as the day before. There we learned from the prisoners that the supplies of gas had unexpectedly run out during the night. We had been spared on account of this accident!"

Helina's story was the most miraculous I'd ever heard, as shortly after that, in the camp she was shot but she managed to survive!

I was keen to include this in the book and tried to get in touch with her. I was thinking afterwards that I was perhaps foolish to think she was still living after all this time. She was living in Poland till after the war and emigrated to Israel in 1947, so, if she was alive and able, there would be little chance she would understand or respond to my English!

Time passed and I had dismissed the vain hope of ever hearing from her, when an email arrived! She also writes poetry and I was absolutely delighted to hear from her! It was such a great privilege and honour and really humbling to get such a lovely message of encouragement about my book that I shall forever treasure!

Speculation
Confrontation
Exclamation
Deportation
Immigration
No Explanation
Agitation
Abomination
Provocation
Humiliation
Deprivation
Victimisation
Infestation
Starvation
Emaciation
Dr Mengele's castration
And experimentation
Illumination
Separation
Condemnation
Suffocation
Obliteration
Furnace Blazing
Finally Liberation
And Salvation
Hope appears in the end

When in Poland, we went to visit a Jewish Community Centre. I chatted with a girl there and shared with her that I was writing a book about the Holocaust. She explained to me that most of the remaining Jewish people don't like to talk about the Holocaust, as that is about death, and they like to focus on living life to the full, whilst respectfully remembering overcoming death by living a vibrant life.

Jewish Community Centre

She said that the Jewish faith is very much based on life, and its tradition encourages them to affirm life and proclaim hope – always – A valuable lesson we could all learn!

(The thief comes only to steal and kill and destroy, I have come that they may have life and have it to the full. John 10 v 10)

CHAPTER NINE

Towards the end of 1944, when the Russian army was rapidly advancing, Himmler had issued two main instructions to the Nazis; firstly, Jews must not be liberated and secondly all evidence of Nazi crimes must be destroyed.

The atmosphere in the camps had changed, but rather than hope rising in those imprisoned there, fear rose as priorities and routines throughout the camps changed. Although there was the welcome sight of some gas chambers and crematorias being blown up, food and water at this time was often denied and many starved to death. The water mains were destroyed in an air raid, making the time prior to liberation particularly harrowing.

The SS were randomly opening fire with machine guns, shooting people on mass, to prevent their liberation and many who had survived all the horrors and extreme hardships of the camps were gunned down just hours before being liberated!
Documents were destroyed and buildings demolished in a frantic effort to cover up all traces of crime.

Between the 17th and the 23rd of January 1945, the prisoners capable of marching, about 6,000, were evacuated and many of them, who had to travel about

70 kilometers on foot, without even stopping for food collapsed and were shot. Those who were so overcome by exhaustion and tried to stop were butchered by pistols or machine gun butts of the SS soldiers escorting them. One hundred and nineteen had been shot within a twenty minute walk for failing to keep up! The S.S guards were armed with machine guns and grenades and their orders were, in the event of a Russian surprise, to kill everyone at once to prevent their liberation. About 7,500 that remained in Auschwitz were liberated by the Soviet army on the 27th January 1945.

This is another memory from Stefania Napiorkowska at the time of the liberation:

"In mid January 1945, when the Red Army was coming close to Lodz, the Germans started to escape from the city. On the 18th January there was a bright, huge glow above the city. The Gestapo wanted to get rid of the evidence of their crimes, so they locked the 4 floors ex-factory building with about 1500 prisoners inside and set fire to it. People were jumping out of the windows, only to be shot by the German soldiers. I went there with my aunt Jagusia a couple days after and the view was much worse than an image of hell itself… Huge piles of burned people lay beside the prison walls, the sickening smell was everywhere... I was only twelve years old when the war started, I am

eighty eight this year and I still cannot understand why people can be such monsters to other ones and I pray to God to save us from another war."
Stefania Napiorkowska

The liberation of the camp at Bergen Belsen was ordered to be filmed by Winston Churchill to be used as evidence on those who had inflicted such horror on the innocent and to bring about convictions of war crimes. Churchill had the most amazing foresight, as there are so many people, like the former Iranian president, Mahmoud Ahmadinejad, who would deny that the Holocaust of the Jews ever happened, while at the same time threatening another! The release of Churchill's footage is yet more proof the Holocaust happened, to silence the deniers!

Churchill

When news came to Churchill's ears
The evidence confirmed his fears
Millions of Jews were murdered dead
Worst world wide massacre, he said
Bomb the chambers? Bomb the tracks?
Or send military in, on ground attacks?
In the West, D-Day Victory songs they sung
While East, lifting the lid on horror began

A documentary was shown on television at the beginning of 2015 to mark the 70th anniversary of the liberation of the Belsen Camp. Prior to that, it was never shown, as it was considered too horrific for viewing.

Watching this was a truly shocking experience for me! The images that I saw impacted my mind, and I was so traumatised by it that I couldn't sleep, so I began to write in order to offload and to try and cope with the nightmare I had witnessed.

The cameraman filming the event, was obviously very experienced at his job, but no amount of expertise could have prepared him for the gruesome scenes that he was to witness from behind his camera lens!

The Camera Man

I would wish to remind the world
That these barbaric camps are true
I'm chosen to film the liberation
Of each remaining Jew
Usually filming dignitary visits
Or a commissioning event
But here to a dreadful death camp
I have now been sent

The choking stench of human flesh
No camera could capture
The horror I witnessed left my mind
Cracked with a permanent fracture
Naked corpses carpeted the camp
Draining the life from the living
Soldiers in tanks with loudspeakers
Instructions they were giving

The film to be used in evidence
To convict the guilty of war crimes
And seventy years later on
To share the truth in your time.

Behind the lens I was in pain
Seventy years on
These images remain.

People in the neighborhood were invited to come and
see what had been going on in the camp nearby where
they lived. Many women were holding hankies to
their noses and collapsing when they caught sight of
the emaciated corpses.

When the children and adults were released, you saw
young children being led out having to walk past all
these corpses lying everywhere, like a scene from a
gruesome horror film, but this was reality!

They paid their own fares
And boarded the train of death
Packed their treasured possessions
For the new life ahead
Hard forced labour and starvation
Crammed in squalor with poor sanitation
Dysentery, typhoid and desperation
Murderers, rapists released to oversee
Commissioned to commit brutality
Paraded naked for selection
Right went back to the labour section
Left to the showers
Never seen again
Disappearing up the forest path
Like the blueish smoke in the aftermath

CHAPTER TEN

Liberation

Before the barb wire
fence of Auschwitz
 came in sight
The stench of death in the air
made the Soviets white
Being hardened to war,
they were accustomed but felled
Nothing prepared them
for what they beheld.

Flesh clinging to frames,
as though vacuum packed
Rotting corpses about
and in piles some were stacked
Babies, boys, girls, men, women, all Jews
All that remained was hair, teeth and shoes

Those who had been marched out prior to the Auschwitz camp being liberated, were taken to other work camps, where some worked in potato fields. Conditions were again terrible, no proper sanitation and very little in the way of food.

Although most of occupied Europe was liberated by April 1945, it wasn't until the 7th of May 1945, that the Germans finally surrendered.

Although now those imprisoned had the freedom for which they had for so long been desperate, the reality of their situation was beginning to sink in.

For most, this was that, since their homes had been bombed, they had nowhere to go, their families were dead, or they had nobody to turn to, no one left to welcome them. Where would they go and what country would be ready to accept them?

The post war relief programme, although welcome, was inefficient and often corrupt. In liberating the concentration camps the Allies, not realising the full extent of what they were facing, were unprepared.

People then died because of lack of proper medical care and because they had difficulties digesting the heavy rich food that was now handed out to them.

Many were placed in temporary accommodation next to where the German military had been, and were lodged three to a room.

In this state of displacement, these Jewish refugees faced total rejection. Countries wouldn't accept them and the majority chose to go to Israel

Their troubles were far from over when they arrived as now the Arabs were out to destroy them! What many of us don't appreciate is that these, weak, traumatised, grief stricken and broken people now had to fight in the 1948 war of independence!

After many years, finally being able to lie in a soft warm bed, with a real pillow under your head instead of your shoes, many could not sleep. They were fearful that the Nazis would return and shoot them all for daring to sleep in their beds.

All these decades later, memories are lodged in their minds like a bullet that no surgeon can remove. Fear still tortures like a poison. The horrors remain fresh in the mind as if it happened yesterday. Nightmares of persecution, cruelty, separation and being chased by Nazis are very present, when aged eyes close.

The Jews who survived the war are driven, they cannot forget and they cannot bear the thought that the world will not remember. As they grow older, it becomes more and more important to them, that no one be permitted to forget. This is what survivors feel they owe their dead loved ones and the means by which survivors hope to prevent history from repeating itself.

One survivor's story, that a small act of unexpected kindness was once shown to him in the camp where he was given some clothing and acknowledged with a smile and a nod. In order to cope with all the everyday horror, he chose to magnify this act of kindness in his mind and focus on that act of goodwill and he refused to let the evil around fill his mind! What a fantastic attitude to have!

In Honor of the Jews

I will write a record, a statement of truth
Europe's vast Jewish population starved to death
Disrespecting the intrinsic value of human life
Failing to even recognise its victims by number
The blades of grass covering this camps shame
Seemed to be considered of greater importance
But the grass withers and the flowers fade
And the word of the Lord endures forever
His chosen people and vengeance is His.

How can police shoot innocent Jews willy nilly
Then walk away without even a twinge of guilt?
In Nazi law killing Jews has no legal consequence
A breeding ground for a culture of cruel depravity

Herded inhumanely to the barbed wire enclosure
Looted, starved, stripped of dignity and belongings
Beaten by the Gestapo and left for dead
With no good Samaritans passing by
Where small birds once sang
Vultures now circle and hover
Transparent skin revealing a shrunken skeletal frame
Yet they sing praise to Jehovah
Till finally silenced by death
They know this is not the end,
It's just the beginning

CHAPTER ELEVEN

There are many people who have an insensitive attitude towards the Holocaust and would like us to forget about it. They try to trivialise what happened and deny its severity.

This is a huge insult, trampling over the cruel injustice inflicted on the survivors, their families and all the millions of countless others that this has had a devastating ripple effect upon. How can we possibly deny the facts or choose to forget the greatest genocide that was inflicted on innocent people?

A British soldier clearing the bodies at the camp at Bergen-Belsen (Courtesy of USHMM photo archives)

I heard an interesting story of a woman who in 2010 was stuck when travelling, during the time the Icelandic Volcano erupted, sending a huge ash cloud over Europe and nobody could fly. Buses and trains couldn't cope with the six million people that were unforeseeably trapped. She asked God why this was happening and He told her that the combination of the ash cloud and the six million affected travellers were a sign that God had not forgotten the six million people turned to ash in the concentration camps of Europe!

" But you have gone too far, killing them without mercy, and all Heaven is disturbed"
(2 Chronicles 28 v 9)

Many people would seek to blame a God they don't even believe in, and refuse to recognise its evil source, that is all too prevalent in this world today. If anti-semitism was right why would God allow His Son, to be born as a Jew?

They say that history repeats itself and that is certainly true. If we look at our first record of Jewish history recorded in the Torah, we see the Jews enslaved in hard labour camps by the Egyptians, under the evil dictatorship of Pharaoh.

Even in our extremely politically correct world today I have been deeply saddened to see that Anti-

Semitism is still very much prevalent in our society.

There are many records of Jews who tried to convert to other religions but that didn't save them. It was the Nazi discrimination against their race enforced by their evil leader Hitler that instigated their annihilation.

Hitler, who just prior to coming to power had been in prison for nine months, a convicted criminal. With his theory that a big lie would be more believable, this was swept along in a sea of deception with his false ideal of creating the perfect race.

Germans, ensnared in deceit were caught up in a trance of false worship, saluting and hailing this criminal.

A recent television documentary exposed Hitler as being a drug addict. He was hopelessly hooked on barbiturates and latterly crystal meth!

A doctor and a pharmacist were interviewed as they looked over Hitler's medical record from his own personal doctor who went everywhere with him as he had become so dependent on him.

Both these medical professionals were shocked at the

dose that he was on of these illegal drugs, and were commenting on the effects that they would be having on his brain!

It is scary to think that a country could be controlled and manipulated by a convicted criminal and drug addict and be taken over by neurotic prejudices, that filter down through generations!

A nation that was hailing Hitler with such dedicated passion and loyalty, this evil dictator, was killing innocent people, children, the elderly and the disabled.

We who are Christians see Jesus, who welcomed children, healed the sick, raised the dead, fed the hungry, taught us to love one another and to help the poor and needy, being mocked, beaten, spat on, with a crown of thorns on His head.
They mocked and hailed Him, "King of the Jews!" Then crucified Him. His last words were, "Father forgive them, for they know not what they do!"

We Christians who are familiar with the suffering our Saviour went through, should feel most acutely the suffering of Jews in the holocaust.

Today were we left with the same choice, life or death – what would we choose? We owe it to our children to discover the truth, not to rely on what the media would have us believe.

Hitler led a nation to believe that through him there would be a perfect race and that resulted in causing the brutal deaths of millions of innocent people.

Is there still an evil deception abounding, trying to keep us from discovering the real truth?

In the end there will be a final selection process that we shall all face, not judged by Dr Mengele, but by Jesus, the obne we Christians call the King of the Jews:

"Then the king will say to those on His right, 'Come you who are blessed by My Father, take your inheritance, the kingdom prepared for you since before the creation of the world. for I was hungry and you gave me something to eat, I was thirsty and you gave me something to drink, I was a stranger and you invited me in, I needed clothes and you clothed me, I was sick and you looked after me I was in prison and you came to visit me.'

Then the righteous will answer Him, 'Lord when did we see You hungry and feed You, or thirsty and give you something to drink? When did we see You a stranger and invite You in, or needing clothes and cloth You? When did we see You sick or in prison and go to visit You?'

The king will reply, 'I tell you the truth, whatever you did for one of the least of these brothers of mine, you did for Me.'

Then He will say to those on His left, 'Depart from Me, you who are cursed, into the eternal fire prepared for the devil and his angels, For I was hungry and you gave Me nothing to eat, I was thirsty and you gave Me nothing to drink, I was a stranger and you did not invite Me in, I needed clothes and you did not clothe Me, I was sick and in prison and you did not look after Me.'

They will also answer, 'Lord when did we see You hungry or thirsty or a stranger, or needing clothes, or sick or in prison and not help You?'

He will reply, 'I tell you the truth, whatever you did not do for the least of these, you did not do for Me.' Then they will go away to eternal punishment, but the righteous to eternal life."

(Matthew 25 v 34 - 46)

From 1947 till today Jews from all over the world have been returning to Israel, as life in other countries has been becoming more and more hostile.

Even today, as we see the conflict in the Middle East, If you spend any time in Israel you will soon come to learn that reports of the conflict are extremely biast and very one sided, why is this?

Why is this twisting of truth gathering momentum and nations turning and siding against Israel, the Jewish nation, haven't they suffered enough?

Life Is Not a Game

It's like a game
Pawns with the Star of David
You inflict with the most punishment and cruelty
As if to gain more points
In this sick political game
Your brainwashed mind
Is programmed with evil
A poison
That drains compassion
Enabling you to deceive
Hundreds and thousands daily
Rounding them in
To your pretend shower blocks
You lock them in
Seal their fate
You ignore their frantic
Pleas for mercy
You pour in the cyclone gas
Till every last cry is silenced.
One day you will face their God
You can't escape that fate

And unless you repent
Your cry for help too will be ignored

"Vengeance is mine," Saith the Lord.

When people are being persecuted like this, there are three responses:-

(1) You can participate in the evil of those inflicting the suffering
(2) You can be indifferent, or
(3) You can stand up for injustice like Oscar Schindler, Irena Sendler, Jane Mailer, the Christian man that risked his life to smuggle Miriam to safety, or the Polish people who dodged SS bullets to give the water to those dying of thirst on the overcrowded cattle trains.

So often we respond with indifference when things don't directly affect us, but for me, knowledge requires a response and my response has been this book.

CHAPTER 12

MIRIAM'S STORY

Common areas in which those who survived struggle with are: fear, identity and guilt that they themselves have survived, when so many, if not all of their families and friends were killed or died of starvation or disease.

This is Miriam's story in her own words.........

"I was well into my fifties before I learned my mother's name."

"My darling aunt, towards the end of her life, was sick and confused, and I was doing my best to take care of her. Waking up in the middle of the night and not knowing where she was and which way was up, she called out 'Rita, Rita'. I came and settled her, this happened several times."

"Needless to say, my name is not Rita, but of course that did not matter."

"A few days later, when my aunt was feeling better, and her mind was clearer, I asked her who Rita was. She looked at me with surprise in her eyes, as if she thought my question was stupid, and snapped: 'Rita was your mother.'

I wanted to ask her how come she had never told me that before, I wanted to rage and shout about the fact that I had to wait until I was fifty eight years old to learn that, but of course I did neither. She was not up to it and neither was I. So I just went into the bathroom and cried.

"Later that day, when we both calmed down a bit, and we were having a pleasant chat, I said: 'I thought my mother's name was Regina.'

"Yes," she said, "it was, officially. But she hated it, and as she was growing up, she made all of us call her Rita. So that's what we did."

"That was the end of the conversation, and my aunt would not say anything else on the subject, then, or any time thereafter."

"I mention this incident to illustrate a curious fact. My aunt and my grandmother never wanted to talk about my dead parents or about anything to do with the war or the holocaust. All I have learned as a child or an adult were either the result of things I have overheard when the conversation was not for my ears, or when I nagged my granny for information so much, that she gave in and dropped a few facts.

"As a matter of fact, I am not even sure that some of those snippets of information were actual facts, or just something my granny invented to get rid of the inquisitive child.

"I was born at the end of 1942, in the middle of the war, in several countries.

"No, my mother did not give birth on a plane flying over Europe, it was just that the international borders kept changing.

"The small town in which I was born was called Munkacs in Hungarian, but even the name has changed since.

"Originally in Hungary in the times of the forgotten peace, before Europe knew either world war, it then became part of the Austro-Hungarian Empire. After the first world war, when the new country of Czechoslovakia was created, my town was ceded to the Slovakian part of that. Then, in the second world war, when Germany and Austria reclaimed territories taken away from them, so did Hungary, and Munkacs became Hungarian again. At the end of the war, when the Red Army "liberated" that region, it also annexed it, and my birthplace became part of the Soviet Union. And now, that the Soviet Union is no longer in existence, Munkacs – or, in Russian, Mukachevo – is in the Ukraine. Even my birth certificate is in two languages: the form is Hungarian but it is filled out in Russian. So I can't even be sure of my name – Kathleen in English, Katalin in Hungarian, Katerina in Russian.

"It is no wonder then that I feel that I have no roots, and no sense of belonging. I am a professional foreigner.

"In Hungary, where I grew up, I was a Jew. In Israel, where I lived as a teenager and a young adult, I was a Hungarian, and was given yet another name: Miriam, translating my middle name, Marianna, to Hebrew. And in Britain, my adopted country, I am simply an alien.

"Yes, I parked my flying saucer around the corner.

"Here come the stories gained mostly from my grandmother. I cannot vouch for their absolute truth, though I do believe them to be mostly factual.

"My wonderful granny died when I was sixteen, and I was not old enough or mature enough to ask enough questions or the right questions to gain all the information I could have or should have had. Neither she, nor my darling aunt wanted to talk about anything involving my parents, their life, their death, the war or the Holocaust.

"I suppose it was just too painful, and they did not wish to inflict that pain on me. They did their best to protect me, but that protection left me naive, ignorant, and unprepared for the pain life inflicts on you anyway.

"So this is how the story goes:

"In early spring 1944, nearly a year and a half old, I lived in the Munkacs ghetto with my mother, my eight year old brother Louis, and my newborn baby sister Eva.

"Lived" may be a bit of an exaggeration, but many people have written about "life" in the ghettos before so there is no need to elaborate.

"My father Sigmund was not there, he had been taken with most other able-bodied Jewish men of Munkacs to a forced labour camp several months beforehand, and he did not even know about the existence of his third child.

"So the ghetto was filled with women, children and old people, and my baby sister was born there. Like in many other cities and towns, the ghetto was in the grounds of a brick factory, and what the many hundreds, thousands of people, lived on, I can't even imagine.

"My grandmother and my aunt lived in Budapest, and they heard rumours about the possibility that the Jews of Munkacs were about to be deported to Auschwitz. How these rumours reached their ears, I have no idea.

"My aunt was then a young, streetwise, decisive woman, and she and my granny decided to do something about it, to try and save the family.

"Munkacs is of course several hundred miles away from Budapest, and Jews were not allowed to travel freely, but my aunt knew somebody, whose brother was a conductor on the train going that way.

"Even though the Jews were not allowed out of the ghetto, Christians from the outside were allowed in to visit, to trade food for money or jewellery.

"So the kind man, carrying a letter from my granny, went into the ghetto to steal out my brother. As he worked on that train just once a week, the plan was to repeat the adventure every week, until he took out the whole family, Louis first, me second, mother and baby last.

"As far as I know, when he got to Munkacs, he hired a small cart or wheelbarrow filled with hay, in order to hide my brother in it, to escape the attention of the guards on his way out, but when he managed to find my family, he discovered that Louis was ill with something like chicken pox, so my mother gave me to him instead.

"He hid me in the wheelbarrow, took me to the train, somehow secreted me there, allegedly drugging me, and on arriving to Budapest, presented me to my aunt.

"When he went back to Munkacs the following week, he was too late. The ghetto was empty, all the Jews of Munkacs had been taken to Auschwitz.

["If the kind reader feels that I am matter of fact and unemotional in describing these events, that is the only way I can do it. As it is, I am shaking while writing this, and being more emotional about it, would drive me to hysterics.]

"The following is not a factual account. I don't know exactly what happened, and there were no witnesses left. But this is how I imagined it every time I could not help thinking about it, and though the details may be wrong, the general outline is no doubt correct.

"On a cold dawn in early April 1944, the thousand or so Jews of Munkacs ghetto were herded to the railway station. The women, children and old people, some of them still in their pyjamas, carried some food and little bundles of belongings, all they could gather in the few minutes they were given between being woken up and setting out.

"There were not too many German guards herding the column, but they were enough, as they were all carrying rifles, using the butts on those who lagged behind. A few old people couldn't keep up, not even with the urging of the rifle butts. When they fell, a sharp crack with a rifle made sure they didn't get up again. And the column continued.

At the station, the train was waiting. Other than the engine, there were only eleven carriages. Ten cattle wagons and, at the rear, a Pullman carriage.

"The doors were open, and it only took a few minutes for the efficient guards to make sure that the wagons were filled, the doors were closed and locked, before they mounted their own carriage and the train started on its way. Rita, Louis and baby Eva were in the second wagon. It was dark inside, as there were no windows, after all, cattle didn't need them. There were two narrow openings high up on each side to let in fresh air, so a little light of the grey dawn did seep in.

"Rita found herself in one corner, right beside two

buckets, one full with water, the other empty. Baby Eva was crying, but Louis, still recovering from his recent illness, felt himself to be the man of the family, and arranged his bundle and his mother's for them to sit on. Rita bared a breast for the baby, and the family huddled together.

"It took the people in the wagon about an hour to discover what the empty bucket was for, when they realised that there were no bathroom facilities. They moved it to the opposite corner and arranged a makeshift curtain around it.

"Then the men moved to one side, turned towards what they figured to be the east, and got on with their morning prayers.

"In the evening the train stopped at a small station. Coal and water were taken on for the engine, and from each wagon one person was allowed out under guard to empty the full bucket and to fill the empty one with water. Night arrived and the people settled down the best they could on the dirty wooden floor for sleep. Most were hungry, many ill, some crying, and a few never to wake again.

"Two more days passed. By the morning of the third, all the food was gone, as was the water, and baby Eva had stopped crying and feeding. But Rita refused to stop cuddling her, and refused to believe in what everybody around her knew. At noon the train stopped for the last time, the doors were opened and all the Jews were told to get off. They didn't know where they were, but the signs said Auschwitz Birkenau, and another announced "Arbeit macht frei".

"They were told to put all their belongings in a pile, and then were separated into two groups. The smaller of the two consisted of young girls and women without children, who were led away to the left. Everybody else, the elderly, the mothers and the children, were directed to the right, towards what the guards said were the wash houses. Rita went with them, holding the dead baby in one arm and, with her other hand, grasping Louis' hand.

"At the doors, they were made to strip, leave their clothes and enter. And the doors closed behind them.

Budapest.

"Of course the Jews were persecuted in Budapest as well. Some Hungarians were always – and are still today – anti-semitic, with many noted exceptions, but these facts are well documented and I need not talk about them.
"But, as I said before, my aunt was a brave and

streetwise woman, and did her best to protect her family.

"Again, I cannot help but mention that neither my aunt nor my granny ever wanted to talk about those days, but a few little details I did manage to gain.

"When I was about twelve, I listened at the keyhole as my aunt and her friend – a survivor of Auschwitz - were talking. And my bad behaviour was rewarded. I learned that, for a while in 1944, my aunt managed to acquire false documents via the Swedish Embassy. According to those my granny was a peasant woman from some obscure part of Hungary, my aunt, her daughter, was a seamstress, and I was her illegitimate daughter. Very brave of her, as in those days having an illegitimate child was a huge shame in any family, and totally unheard of among Jews. But she dared anything to save us.

"Of course everybody has heard of that saint, the Swedish diplomat Raoul Wallenberg, who helped save thousands of Budapest's Jews by issuing them with faked documents and by housing many of them in safe houses. (Wallenberg's good deeds were 'rewarded' by imprisonment by the Russians and he allegedly died in a Russian prison two years after the end of the war.)

"How or when it happened, how it worked and how

long it lasted, I do not know. I also don't know and have often wondered, on what the Jews in hiding – and people in wartime in general - actually lived on. I suppose I will never find out. Also at about the same time, as my thirst for knowledge – or maybe just my curiosity - was growing, I decided to learn German.

"My grandmother's mother tongue was German (remember the Austro-Hungarian Empire?), and when the two of them wanted to discuss something "not for the child's ears", they reverted to that language. So in total secrecy I started to study.

"By that time I did have some experience in learning a foreign language – having been taught Russian in school – so I did have some idea how to go about it. And because my motivation was strong, I learned very fast indeed.

"For over a year I managed to keep my newly acquired knowledge hidden, and learned many so-called secrets. Most of them were totally trivial and now forgotten. But I do remember one snippet. Apparently, when I was about two, at the time when we were supposed to be a Catholic family, I nearly caused our downfall. Somebody visiting our family pulled out a yellow handkerchief from his pocket, and I piped up: 'That would make a great yellow star.'

"In those days all Jews were supposed to wear a yellow star on their lapels to announce to the world their ethnic belonging, and a toddler knowing that fact could have only been part of a Jewish family.
The visitor must have been a very good man indeed not to denounce us to the authorities.

"But my search for the truth started much earlier than the age of twelve, and this is something I still remember very well. I must have been six or seven years old when, in school, we were learning about professions. The teacher called us one by one, and asked us what our parents did.

"When my turn came, she asked me what my father's job was. I said I didn't have a father. She asked if my parents were divorced which, in those days, was not such a regular occurrence. I said no. So she asked, with pity in her eyes, if my father was dead. I said no, I never had a father. I simply did not realise that a child was supposed to have a mother and a father. As a matter of fact, though of course I was aware of the existence of men, I did not know a single one intimately. I lived with my aunt and granny, thinking that my aunt was my mother. I went to a girls' school. My teachers were women, and our narrow social circle did not include any men either. So the teacher told me to sit down, and then wrote a note, gave it to me, and told me to give it to my 'mother'.

"I did not witness the meeting between the two of them, but as a result, a few days later, my aunt and granny sat me down, and told me that my real parents were dead, that my granny was my mother's mother, that my 'mother' was my mother's sister and thus my aunt. And that was that, nothing more was said and nothing changed.

"And that was where my search for the truth started. My friend Eva, with whom I have so much in common that I call her 'my sister' by different parents", and who knows about my background, once asked me a difficult question: 'Do you ever feel guilty about the fact that you survived instead of your brother?' And I had to admit to her – and to myself – that yes, I do.

"People talk about 'survivor guilt'. It might be difficult to understand, but yes, I tend to feel guilty about the fact that I survived and the rest of my family didn't. And the only way to alleviate that guilt is to achieve something great that may justify my survival.

"I was born clever, but somebody wise once said: 'Being born clever is like being born with big feet. It is just an accident of birth, and it is what you do with it that makes a difference.'

"Well, I had done nothing with it. I have not discovered the cure for cancer or the common cold, I had added nothing to world literature. I have made nothing or done anything that altered the human condition, and I didn't even have children to carry on the family name. Perhaps my brother would have won the Nobel Peace Prize.

"So yes, even though I know that the death of my family is no way my fault, I feel guilty.

"Much though I may be sad about my family having been murdered in the holocaust, I am even more upset about the fact that their life left no trace. I have no birth certificate, no death certificate, no grave to visit. It is as if they never existed.

"So when, after my retirement, I bought a computer, one of the first things I did, was to contact Yad Vashem, and added the names of my family to the long-long list of those lost in the Holocaust. That list is not complete, it never could be complete, as whole families were totally wiped out, leaving nobody who could put their names on the list.

"I have contacted Yad Vashem once before, when I was just twenty, in the hope that they may find for me some long-lost relation of whose existence I was unaware, as even my granny knew nothing, or claimed to know nothing about my father's side.

"They did their best, but the task was futile, as I did not have any information for them to use as a starting point. I don't know where and when my father was born, so even though Yad Vashem found many people with my surname, they were all of Polish origin. Yes, they may be distant relations, but I had no way of knowing. About eight years ago I finally got an opportunity to make a difference.

"At the insistence of my friends, I visited Hungary for the first time since I left at the age of sixteen. Among other places,I went to see Budapest's main synagogue, now a World Heritage site. I remembered it from my childhood, but it has been renovated since and is absolutely beautiful.

"The reason it survived the second world war and the German occupation, is that it was then used as a holding pen for many thousands of Jews before they were taken to be shot dead. This was in the last few weeks of the war, when the Nazis were in too much of a hurry to take them to Auschwitz.

"The synagogue now has a Holocaust museum and a courtyard with a huge metal tree with many thousands of bronze leaves, each signifying one life of a Jew lost in the Holocaust. This gave me an opportunity of which I was not aware before. I made arrangements and paid for two new leaves, and now the names of my family are marked on that tree.

"So yes, my family did exist, and they live as leaves on that tree, as well as in my heart.

The tree Of Life

Cry for those who mourn in Zion
Beneath the weeping willow tree
Its leaves remember loved ones
Tears drop with every memory

I have been so moved by Miriam's story and am so grateful to her for allowing me to include it in this book.

Appendix

A Survivor

Over seventy years on, still survivors lives are halted by the Holocaust. Cecile Klein powerfully describes for us how it has affected her:

"A survivor is an actor experienced in her art. She puts on nice clothes, matched up with a smile, and tries to recapture the pleasures of life, and becomes keenly aware of her inability to enjoy. A survivor will go on vacation and, while watching a show, there will appear in her mind the picture of her mother with her grandson in her arms gasping for breath.

A survivor will read in the paper about a fire, and desperately hope that her brother died from the fumes before the fire reached him.

A survivor will go to a party and feel lonesome in the crowd.

A survivor will be very quiet, yet scream inside.

A survivor will cry, and pretend to her children it's a mere headache.

A survivor will make large weddings, invite a great many people, but the ones she wants most will never arrive.

A survivor will go to a funeral and not cry for the one who died, but for the ones who were never buried.

A survivor will reach out to you and not let you

get close, for you remind her too much of the difference between her and you, remind her too much of what could have been, yet will never be.

A survivor is only at ease with other survivors, though they never talk about their past.

A survivor is broken and beaten in spirit; she lies even to herself and pretends to be like you.

A survivor is a wife, mother, friend, neighbor, yet unknown to all, she is only known to herself.

A survivor possesses one thing you do not; a fearlessness of death, for she has faced death so many times, and also because she knows that this is when she will finally find peace.

To understand, that when they killed the six million, you might as well know what happened to the living. This you cannot study in your textbooks, our pain is not on record. It's important for you to know, since you are at the threshold of your life. Some of you may become future leaders; it will be up to you to fight oppression and bigotry.

You must insist on laws where everybody is free to worship, to lead productive lives, and to educate their children. If you remember the Holocaust, you will prevent history from repeating itself. You must never again stand by silently when such injustice breaks out against a people."

(An extract from Holocaust Poetry by Cecilie Klein. Thanks to Gefen Publishing House, Jerusalem.)

While every effort was made to trace the owners of copyrighted material, the author would like to apologise for any omissions and will be pleased to incorporate any missing acknowledgments in any future editions.